The Rescue of Daniel

WestBow Press books may be ordered through booksellers or by contacting:

WestBow Press
A Division of Thomas Nelson & Zondervan
1663 Liberty Drive
Bloomington, IN 47403
www.westbowpress.com
1 (866) 928-1240

ISBN: 978-1-9736-4343-2 (sc)
ISBN: 978-1-9736-4344-9 (e)

Library of Congress Control Number: 2018912905

Print information available on the last page.

WestBow Press rev. date: 10/27/2018

WESTBOW
PRESS®
A DIVISION OF THOMAS NELSON
& ZONDERVAN

The Rescue of Daniel

Kay Bretton

Once long ago, in a faraway land,
   was a king named Darius who needed a hand
   with ruling his kingdom which was given to him,
   for alone his chances of succeeding were slim.

To protect his kingdom from suffering loss
   Darius chose Daniel to be a boss.
He chose two more bosses to serve with Danny
   and soon Dan's predicament became **quite uncanny.**

For because Dan was good and because he was wise
  Daniel was favored in King Darius' eyes.
It wasn't long before Dan got more power
  and the other two bosses got **more mad by the hour!**
They soon decided to come up with a plan
  which would once and for all get rid of old Dan.
Now Daniel was faithful---an honest sort.
They couldn't find a reason to take him to Court.

But then they remembered about **Daniel's God!**
For they knew he refused to bow or to nod
   to any other idol or man
    and they thought that truly they had a good plan.
Off to King Darius the whole group did go.
The poor king was tricked for he really didn't know
   that these evil persons were after old Dan
    with their **sneaky, despicable, deceitful plan.**

Then addressing the king they spoke, "We agree
   that it would be proper if you would decree
   that from this moment on it is no longer **lawful;**
   in fact, you should warn that it would be **awful**
   for anyone to bow on his knees
   and to talk, or pray, or make any pleas
   to any other God or man
   except you, **oh King."** (They were trapping poor Dan.)

King Darius was flattered and thought, **"This is good.**
Let it be written just as it should.
The penalty set if one disobeys:
   a free trip to the lions' den for thirty days."
Then the king signed his name and it became law.
He didn't think of Daniel a bit---**not at all!**

But back at his house Dan was down on his knees
    kneeling as usual to God with his pleas.
Dan prayed and gave thanks to the **Almighty One.**
He just went on praying as he always had done.
Now what do you think that those evil men did?
Well, they **slunk and they slithered and some say they slid**
    right to old Dan's place to catch him in prayer.
They wanted him punished **right then and right there!**

Then to the king those nasty ones ran.
They simply **couldn't wait** to get rid of old Dan.
King Darius was saddened when he saw through their trick
    for punishing Daniel **just made him sick!**
He paced back and forth trying to think of a way
    to rescue poor Daniel that very day.
The trap had been set by those **evil** men
    when back to the king they went once again
    to remind him that Daniel had disobeyed
    for to his God he had faithfully prayed.

Now Darius knew that Daniel could trust
    in the God of his prayers for He really is just.
He proclaimed to Daniel with words very true,
    "The God that you serve will deliver you!"
Then into the lions' den Daniel was cast
    and the evil men watching were having a **blast!**
For they rolled a stone in front of the cave
    thinking, "No way could anyone possibly save
    old Dan from becoming a meal very fine
    for more than one hungry, ferocious feline."

Meanwhile, the king couldn't sleep and couldn't eat,
So that very last morning **he must have been beat!**
At daybreak, when it began to be light,
he ran 'til the lions' den was in his sight.
As he approached it to come up near
he cried with a voice that trembled in fear.
He shouted quite frightened and lacking in nerve
"Oh Dan, was the God that you constantly serve
able to protect you from this horrible thing?"
Then Daniel replied, **"Long live the King!!!!**
For an angel of God held the lions' mouths shut.
My Lord really got me out of this rut!!!"

So Daniel was injured not one little bit
   and king Darius was very pleased over it!
Now those **evil, nasty, despicable men**
   were **themselves** thrown into the lions' den.

Then Darius, the King, made another decree
   that the God of Daniel forever would be.
For he delivers and rescues and does wonders and signs
   as surely as Daniel was delivered from lions!

Daniel, Chapter 6: 1-28

Author Biography

Born and raised in northwestern Pennsylvania, Kay Bretton graduated from Edinboro University of Pennsylvania with a degree in elementary education. She later received her master's in counseling from Liberty University in Virginia. The majority of her adult life has been spent in Florida where she has been devoted to working with children, teens, and adults in a variety of educational and counseling settings. With a lifetime interest in writing, she has a deeply held belief that it is important for children to read, or have read to them, stories that reinforce Christian principles and values. She believes that rhyming and humor greatly enhance the process of learning and committing to memory, and she has therefore chosen that format for her stories.

Printed in the United States
By Bookmasters